PRAYING
ALWAYS

PRAYING ALWAYS

☆

Frans Bakker

☆

Translated by Cornelis and Fredrika Pronk

The Banner of Truth Trust

THE BANNER OF TRUTH TRUST
3 Murrayfield Road, Edinburgh EH12 6EL
PO Box 621, Carlisle, Pennsylvania 17013, USA

*

*This book, originally entitled 'Facets of Prayer', was first published in
The Netherlands by B. V. Uitgeverij 'De Banier', Utrecht.*

*English translation edited by Baker Book House, USA, copyright 1981
Reprinted 1984
First reprinted by the Banner of Truth Trust
with the title 'Praying Always' 1987*

ISBN 0 85151 514 2

*

*Reproduced, printed and bound in Great Britain by
Hazell Watson & Viney Limited,
Member of the BPCC Group,
Aylesbury, Bucks*

Foreword

Frans Bakker was born March 19, 1919, in Zeeland, the Netherlands. He lost both parents when he was only a young child and thus became acquainted with grief early in life. Brought up by relatives, he developed into a serious young man who learned early to seek the Lord. He loved to read the Bible, and zealously studied the doctrines of the church. Frans was a leader of young people. They profited much from his unusual knowledge of God's Word and spiritual things. But Bakker was not satisfied with such part-time service. It was his burning desire to give himself completely to the Lord's service as a minister of the Word. Not until he was thirty-seven years old was his dream fulfilled. His first congregation was Huizen where he was ordained in 1956. Three years later he accepted a call to Driebergen, where he labored until his death in 1965.

Rev. Frans Bakker was not a great orator, yet many people loved his preaching because of its simplicity and depth. These two characteristics may seem to be mutually exclusive, but they were not in this case. Bakker's sermons were plain and direct, so that even children could follow him most of the time. Yet they were at the same time profound and experiential, so that long-time Christians were also instructed and fed.

Humbleness and seriousness permeated everything he did, whether in the pulpit or visiting his flock. As often happens with men of similar graces and gifts, Bakker died at a relatively young age. His ministry, though richly blessed, was brief. The Lord gave this choice vessel only eight years to labor in His vineyard. While in Driebergen he was stricken with cancer, and although after surgery he recovered for a time so that he could preach again, the dreaded disease returned and gradually destroyed the young preacher's body. But Bakker's spirit was not broken. He at first found it difficult to accept the devastating news that he had cancer, but the Lord enabled him after a brief and fearful struggle to say, "Thy will be done." Knowing himself to be in the tender hands of his faithful Savior, he learned to say with the psalmist, "My soul is even as a weaned child." In spite of much suffering, the period in the hospital and later on his bed at home proved to be a very blessed time both for him and his wife. And not only for them; many friends who visited him came away blessed and comforted. He had an encouraging word for all as he testified of the Lord's goodness to a poor sinner. Toward the end of his life, all fear of death was removed and boldly he could say, "I am ready for the journey." A few days before his death the whole congregation came two at a time to say good-bye to their beloved pastor. Many tears were shed as he spoke lovingly but also solemnly about the need for faith in Christ. He passed away on January 2, 1965.

The book, *Facets of Prayer*, was published during Rev. Frans Bakker's lifetime and has been reprinted many times since his death. As many Dutch readers have been blessed by these deeply spiritual and heart-searching reflections, we thought it wise to make the book available to the English-speaking public. We sincerely hope and pray that the Lord may bless this unusual book on a subject about which we all need so much instruction.

Cornelis Pronk

Contents

PRAYER THAT IS:

Contents

1

Secret

"But thou, when thou prayest, enter into thy closet, and when thou hast shut thy door, pray to thy Father which is in secret; and thy Father which seeth in secret shall reward thee openly" (Matt. 6:6).

At the bottom of man's existence is a deep sense of loneliness. When we honestly search our hearts we must admit with the poet of Psalm 25, "I am desolate."

Our deepest loneliness stems from the fact that we are without God in this world. Ever since the gates of Paradise closed behind us, we have gone our own lonely way. We are alone in this life and are certainly alone in death. In our deepest afflictions we have no refuge; we cannot even help each other when the great enemy, death, strikes. Yet by grace, there is also another kind of solitude, the solitude of the closet, where God's child experiences secret communion with God in prayer. This solitude is to be preferred above all the friendship of the world. Even if in the closet we experience how miserable we are in God's sight, it still is the best place that man can find on earth.

In the days when Christ walked on earth there was much ignorance about secret prayer. Certainly people prayed; the Pharisees even stood on street corners to pray. But alas, it was only a show for the benefit of the people who saw them. No doubt the people who saw the Pharisees pray thought well of their prayers. But the Pharisees didn't understand that prayer is a matter between God and the soul alone. True prayer consists of a relationship between two—God and the sinner.

"But thou," said Christ, "enter into thy closet." This is a lesson we need to learn in our day. What will it profit us to have great gifts of public prayer if we have no knowledge of an intimate relationship with God? Indeed, no matter who we are, if we haven't personally learned what it is to pray, we will meet an unknown God after death.

Do prayer closets exist today? These words are not addressed to the world. We all know that there are no bended knees there. But we are addressing those who from childhood have known that there is a God in heaven who hears prayer. Do you still have closets?

Obviously Christ does not mean a separate room in our home Even there a truly prayerful heart can be lacking. But the question is: "Is there still true prayer?" Do we have a secret and personal fellowship with the Lord? Are there places in our home, even a basement or attic, where the golden cord of prayer is the means of fellowship between heaven and earth? Such prayer brings heaven to earth. This may happen even at work. Nehemiah prayed while he spoke with the king.

We do not overstate when we say that there is no spiritual life if the activity of secret prayer is missing. Prayer is the breath of the soul. Just as the body cannot live without breathing, so the soul cannot live without prayer. A mineworker will die if contact with outside air is cut off. So it is in spiritual life when there is no communication with heaven. If there is no prayer, the soul cannot breathe. It is by prayer that the soul has communion with God.

"Enter into thy closet, and when thou hast shut the door. . . ." Yes, the door must be shut; the door of the hustle and bustle of this world, the door of hypocrisy—all the doors which can hinder true prayer. The door must be closed, for everything here is so tender and intimate. Here a husband cannot tolerate the presence of his wife and here the wife wants to be alone. Here a son or a daughter hides from parents what he or she confesses to the all-knowing God. Here before

God's countenance, everyone is alone with God. Here the right attitude is one of being spiritually uncovered in our shame and misery, exposing our sin and guilt and being stripped of our righteousnesses before the all-seeing God.

Behind those closed doors the sinner experiences the first and the last struggles he will ever have. Here the heart is poured out before God. Here the sometimes tongue-tied do not lack words. Here the most learned speak the language of a child. Here no prayer is too short or too long. Here it sometimes is impossible to stop pleading at the throne of grace; and here, too, one sigh or groan is more than a thousand words. Here you can confess to God what you cannot entrust to man. The Lord knows those who are · His: their names are known to Him; their tears are kept in His bottle; their sighs are laid on His heart. He knows of their struggles. He knows their distress. He listens to each of His children personally as if He had only one child on the whole earth. Here one who truly prays is known by Him.

Christ Himself has given His church the example of praying in secret. How often He went to pray alone on a mountain. But He had nothing to tell the Father which needed to be hidden from others. He did not have a single secret sin to confess. How much more, then, do sinners need the closet! We have much to acknowledge that others should not know and struggles that others do not understand.

To the Pharisee, who in the eyes of the people had such gifts of prayer, it shall one day be said, "I never knew you." The Pharisee had never been really alone with God. Of those who pray in secret it is said: "And thy Father which seeth in secret shall reward thee openly."

In the day of days it will come to light who prayed in secret, even though now they only sigh. Even if now they hardly dare call God their Father, they will not then meet an unknown God, for this God will be the same God they met in their closet.

The Lord will make a separation between those who pray hypocritically and those who pray sincerely. The first shall be amazed that they are not counted with the sheep. They shall say, "Have we not called on thy name on earth?" The latter will be forever amazed because they are not counted with the goats. In that day all things will come to light—all hypocrisy and all truth. Then many first shall be last and many last, first.

To be sure, this life of prayer does not always function actively from day to day. It does not function automatically, for it is so tender and so intimate. At times the heart can be cold and prayerless. Heaven can seem so closed that no prayer seems to penetrate.

Those who truly pray will more and more shamefully and painfully learn that they cannot pray. Yet they will not exchange even the unhappiness experienced in the closet for all the joys of the world. Unhappiness here is preferred to the happiness of the world. Daniel would rather go into the lion's den than leave his prayer closet.

Reader, do you have a closet? If the floors of your home could speak, would they witness to bended knees? Do you dare call the walls of your home to witness to your prayer life? If the doors could speak, would they be able to testify that you have shut them to go into your prayer room? Be honest. What could the walls and doors say about you? Remember that the Lord requires truth in the inward parts. Therefore this is a matter known only to God and you.

"But," says someone, "can you already be assured of your salvation if you know these secret places?" We will say more about this in subsequent chapters, but for now we say that matters are in a sorry state indeed if this seeking of God in secret is not known by you; for then even the first signs of spiritual life are missing. God, your creator, has given you knees to bend, hands to fold, and a mouth to call on Him.

In addition to bended knees you need a prayerful heart. By nature this is not found with any of us. But that does not change the truth that those who neglect prayer will have to acknowledge, "I would not," when they are lost. No one is lost because he asked too much of God, but only because he asked too little, even if it is only a prayer for a prayer, as the disciples asked: "Lord, teach us to pray."

16

What is a church without prayer? No more than an army without weapons. Prayer is the power of the church of God. Alas, it is also the weakness of the church, because among God's people there is so often no time, no desire, and no prayerful heart. Oh, this awful condition of prayerlessness! What backsliding it can cause in the life of grace, especially when compared to the time of first love, when the Lord's help was continually needed and sought. Often a child of God has to look back to that time in shame. How often you now pass the door of the closet, whereas you used to enter it!

Do we not have a continuing need for grace? Is it not true that we live by grace alone? Surely, a cause of much spiritual darkness is lack of prayer. "When I kept silence," says David, "my bones waxed old through my roaring all the day long." His mouth was silent, but his heart cried out. Under this silence the soul seems to be consumed. Yet God has said in His Word, "Pour out your whole heart before me," no matter how cold, how unwilling, and how evil that heart is.

There was a son who began to be in want. But he could still come to his father every day for food. On a certain day he asked his father if he could not get a week's supply at once. This would be much easier and he wouldn't have to come back every day. But his father said, "No, I like to see you come every day." Much more God the Father likes to see His child come to the throne of grace every day. The Lord's people do not receive a store of provisions. It is the same as with the widow of Zarephath. When Elijah said to her that God would keep her alive, no provisions of bags of flour and crocks of oil were sent. Every day she had to live from a handful of flour and a little bit of oil. They stayed as poor in Zarephath as they had been before. But their poverty was turned into wealth. They were poor, yet rich; having nothing, yet possessing everything. Where else is this taught but in secret, in the closet?

That may be why so many of God's people are poor. Poverty often brings dependence on God, while riches tend to nurture an independent spirit. If God's church would spend more time in secret places, how much more tenderness, humility, love, instruction, strength, and light would be experienced! How much more power would radiate from the church! When Moses had been with the Lord, his face shone because of the glory of God. Moses was favored with special grace. But when even the least child of God has been with Him, others will notice.

How blessed are those times of solitude, of being alone with God! There something is received which the world cannot give. One man said on his deathbed that he would not meet a strange, unknown God. Where had he met God? He had learned to know this God in secret, in the closet.

2

Persevering

*"And, behold, a woman of Canaan came out
of the same coasts, and cried unto him, saying,
Have mercy on me, O Lord, thou son of David;
my daughter is grievously vexed with a devil.
But he answered her not a word. And his disciples came and besought him, saying, Send her
away; for she crieth after us. But he answered
and said, I am not sent but unto the lost sheep
of the house of Israel. Then came she and worshipped him, saying, Lord help me. But he
answered and said, It is not meet to take the
children's bread, and to cast it to dogs. And she
said, Truth, Lord: yet the dogs eat of the crumbs
which fall from their master's table. Then Jesus
answered and said unto her, O woman, great
is thy faith: be it unto thee even as thou wilt.
And her daughter was made whole from that
very hour" (Matt. 15:22-28).*

Sometimes we beg the Lord for help, yet receive no immediate answer. Prayer seems to bounce back to earth; there is no answer—and that while the need is so great!

The woman of Canaan experienced this. Her need was very great, for her daughter was grievously vexed with the devil's power. Who can imagine what it is to be the mother of such a child, to look on helplessly while your child's body is cast to and fro by hellish powers? The woman heard that Jesus was in the country of Tyre and Sidon where she lived, so she went to Him with her great need. When she found Jesus she begged, "O Lord, thou son of David, have mercy on me."

She must already have tried many things to obtain healing for her daughter. This physician was her last hope. She poured out her whole heart before Him—and hasn't the Lord said in His Word, "Pour out your heart before me"? But what a disappointment! Christ didn't answer her!

Here was a praying mother and a silent Jesus. All her hope was fixed on Him, but He who is able to help apparently did not want to help. He asked a man who was sick for thirty-eight years, "Wilt thou be made whole?" when that man did not even ask for healing, and now He acted as though He didn't hear or see this woman.

This woman's situation is not an isolated case. The psalmist, too, cried out, "Thou dost not answer!" If our prayer concerned only temporal matters, it would be possible to submit to God's wisdom. But can it be that the Lord doesn't answer immediately when our prayer concerns eternal matters?

Perhaps you have experienced this too. You pray, but see no light. You seek, but don't find. You knock, but no door opens. The longer God's silence lasts, the greater the need becomes. Not one word comes from heaven, and you cry like Job: "O that God would answer me!"

The disciples, anxious to send the woman away, were on her side and wanted Christ to help her. But what does it help if man is on your side, if God is against you? Christ here went against the request of His disciples. "He answered and said, I am not sent but unto the lost sheep of the house of Israel."

What could the woman of Canaan do now? We would think that she would certainly go home. She had heard Christ say that He was sent to the lost sheep of Israel, but she was a heathen. But she did not return home! True need cannot be repressed, for there is nowhere else to go.

Some people say that they have prayed enough already, and so they stop. This proves that the need of the soul does not weigh heavy enough. Those who have a true need cannot stop; they would rather die at the feet of Christ than stop.

P.A.—2

So it was with this woman. We read, "Then came she and worshipped him." She came to Christ and worshiped at His feet so that He could not proceed on His way. She had said so much already, that now she could only say, "Lord, help me!"

Maybe you understand this woman. Perhaps you have, like her, often made your misery and wretchedness known to God. Many words are often laid at the throne of grace—many words, and not one answer. Finally you have no more words and your cry becomes only, "Lord, help me!" Only a cry, a groan, a sigh remains.

We would expect that the greater than Joseph could not control Himself any longer and must reveal Himself to her. Could He who wept at Lazarus' grave and who was moved with inward compassion over the multitude, refuse this woman any longer?

The situation worsened for the woman as Jesus told her that it was not right to take the children's bread and cast it to the dogs. In other words, His healing power was for others, but not for her.

The closet can become so dark. Nothing is worse than a silent God. And what if then the Lord begins to speak of justice instead of grace? What if the answer is: "I cannot do it for your sake"? Then we learn that in ourselves we have no rights; only God has rights.

What did the woman of Canaan do? Did she become bitter? Did she say, I am no worse than others? Did she perhaps say, "Can I help it that I am a heathen?" Or was she offended because she was called a dog? Nothing like that happened! She agreed with what Christ said. She agreed that she had no rights. She acknowledged her unworthiness and sinfulness. Listen to her reply; "Truth, Lord." When she was called a dog and not a child she agreed that it was true. "Truth, Lord"—that is the right attitude of prayer. That is where the Lord wants His people. They will speak well of God, even though it seems that it is a lost cause for them. They may have much boldness and perseverance in their prayers, but they dare not impose on God's justice. When their unworthiness is mentioned they will admit: "Truth, Lord."

Scripture says, "Ask and ye shall receive; knock and it shall be opened unto you; seek and ye shall find." No one has ever found that this is not so. But between the prayer and the answer lies the sovereignty of God. The lesson which a silent heaven teaches is that God is not under any obligation to a sinner. Grace teaches the sinner to beg for grace.

What did the woman of Canaan do next? She didn't give up; she held on. To what? To a crumb which she hoped might fall from the Lord's table. "Yet," she said, "the dogs eat of the crumbs which fall from their masters' table." In other words she was saying, "Lord, let the bread be given to the children of Israel. If I may have only the crumbs, I will be satisfied." One crumb from God, one ray of His light, one mark of His favor would be sufficient. The least favor of heaven is sufficient for people who pray like her.

What had this woman done? She had taken hold of Christ in His own words. She caught Him in what He had said to her. Jesus had spoken of the dogs who were given the leftovers, and thus set the door ajar. Her perseverance serves for instruction in secret prayer and encouragement for poor supplicants.

But of far greater importance is the question, "What did Christ do?" The Savior allowed Himself to be caught in His own words. With His left hand He cast her away, but with His right hand He held on to her. With the one hand He took away her courage and with the other hand He drew her to Himself. The Lord still works this way. He lets us see the impossibility from our side to make room for the possibility on God's side.

Christ said to her, "O woman, great is thy faith!" He could say this to her because she had such great thoughts of God and such small thoughts of herself. She expected much from little and, in her extremity, she clung to Jesus.

From that very hour her daughter was made whole. The woman of Canaan could not yet see this, but faith cannot doubt. Where the Lord speaks there is certainty, and no one, whatever his state of assurance, has ever asked when God speaks, "Is it really true?"

This history is written for discouraged strugglers who ask themselves whether God's blessings can ever be for them, whose fear increases as heaven remains silent. Do you feel your need before God? If it would be said to you, "Be it unto thee even as thou wilt," what would happen? Maybe nothing, because you never laid any needs before the Lord. But what blessed encouragement there is here for unworthy sinners! It is always easier to believe this for others than for yourself. By rights you belong outside. Nevertheless, take courage and keep on, no matter how impossible and hopeless your prayer seems to be! Learn from the woman of Canaan to lay hold on God's Word.

God cannot answer you because of your worthiness and your prayers. But He can do it because of what He has said in His Word—for His own name's sake—because of Christ. That is your pleading-ground and not anything in yourself. When it is a lost cause from your perspective, there is hope that it is a good cause from God's perspective. Your prayer will then be, "Lord, isn't it possible for Thy sake?" What a miracle of grace that this God lets Himself be found and lets Himself be held by His own words! This God is not like man who often forgets or takes back his words! The experience of a silent heaven can be of great benefit for the child of God. Often more is learned in the darkness than in the light. If prayers would always be answered immediately, we would think that it was because we pray so well. Then we would look for grounds in our prayers and see merits in ourselves. It is necessary that the Lord shows His sovereignty; and that with all our praying and knocking and seeking, we see that we have nothing and are nothing, unless we become the objects of God's good pleasure in Christ. In that sense God speaks in His silence. He speaks of His righteousness and of our unrighteousness, because sinners have to end up finally at Christ's feet.

If there ever was one on earth who experienced a silent God, it was Christ on the cross. He cried out under a silent heaven that God had forsaken Him. His perseverance brought Him no relief. He took hold of God, but God let Him go. He was not rejected by God's one hand and drawn close by the other hand, as the woman of Canaan experienced. No, He was cast away by both of God's hands, for He had to pay for all the sins of His own.

In all this He also had to say, "Truth, Lord." And He did say it, for He did not want to take anything away from God's holy justice. For Him there was no crumb from the Lord's table. He became less than a dog, so that there would be everlasting bread for heathens. That is the divine lesson heaven teaches us when it remains silent.

26

There is no worthiness in those who pray, not even in their persevering prayers. Even if every year of your life you would call day and night—without Christ—God would have to be silent forever. It is only because of the drawing love of Christ that a sinner cannot stay away from the throne of God. Therefore, looking back, the saved say, "Lord, I did not take hold of Thee, but Thou didst take hold of me." And therefore they can also sing:

> With joy the meek shall see my soul restored,
> Your heart shall live, ye saints that seek the Lord;
> He helps the needy and regards their cries,
> Those in distress the Lord will not despise.

3

Improper

"Ye ask, and receive not, because ye ask amiss,
that ye may consume it upon your lusts"
(James 4:3).

Things were not right in the congregation
to which James addressed this letter. The people
had faith, but it was a faith without works. James
calls this dead faith, implying that there was also
something wrong with their prayer life.

We know prayer was still practiced because
our text says, "Ye ask." But it was improper
prayer—"ye ask amiss." By that James means
your prayers don't achieve their purpose. No
sweet savor of prayer ascends to the throne of
grace; your prayer gets stuck before it reaches its
goal because it is an abominable smell to God.
Many people have a regular prayer life and they
also persevere in prayer, but their prayers will

never be answered because their attitude of prayer is not right, even though they believe it is.

The closet itself does not make one pray in truth, and prayer—even much prayer—is not always proof of true spiritual life. In the closet there are foolish virgins who do the same as the wise virgins, but who lack the true spirit of prayer. In spite of their faith and their prayers, the situation was not good in the congregation addressed by James. There was much wrong with their daily conduct and the life of prayer cannot flourish where there is an ungodly walk of life.

The poor were oppressed by the rich. They had departed far from the good communism of the time of Pentecost, when the rich sold their goods to help the poor. Now it was the opposite; the rich took advantage of the poor. There were also many "masters." Everyone thought he knew best. They were not poor in spirit, because meek people do not think highly of themselves. These "masters" were experts at breaking the truth up into various doctrines while they forgot that they themselves had to be broken down. They certainly had not learned to practice the doctrine that Christ taught His church when He said, "Learn of me; for I am meek and lowly of heart."

"Wars and fightings" were not uncommon because where man, though a child of God, thinks he knows everything, there will be wars and fights, there will be schisms and trampling of each other underfoot. And the worst thing is that man will think he is fighting the good fight of faith. But the fight of faith is something quite different from waging a civil war. The fight of faith remains and will remain as long as the militant church is on earth. In the fight of faith man loses himself, while in "war" he only builds himself up.

Of such our text says, "Ye ask." If only for once these rich, these masters, and these rebels wouldn't know how to pray, the situation would be quite different. They thought they prayed well, in spite of the fact that their prayer life did not influence their daily conduct. James 4:2 says that they asked not, because actually this was not praying at all.

It was once said of a certain farmer that he was converted by God. "How do you know?" someone asked. The reply was, "He doesn't beat his horses any more." How shall anyone approach the throne of God and at the same time hurt his fellowman, causing worse than physical pain? "If a man says, I love God, and hateth his brother, he is a liar," says Scripture. These liars can be so hard-hearted that they do not notice it themselves and they keep right on praying. What do they pray for and for what purpose do they ask? James says, "that ye may consume it upon your lusts." We pray amiss when we have not died to self and we desire things of God which concern only our self—our self-interest, our self-esteem, and everything else that concerns self—even in spiritual matters.

Think, for example, of Esau. As big and tough as he was, he lay crying bitterly at his father's feet, begging for a blessing. Alas, Esau was concerned with the benefits and not the benefactor. The question is, for what do we pray and what would we do with it if our request was granted? "That ye may consume it upon your lusts." Here we find someone who is not on his knees praying to God. Actually, the reverse is happening. God is put off His throne and man expects God to bow before king "I," who has taken over the throne. That is praying improperly.

James calls such people adulterers and adulteresses. An adulteress doesn't care where her reward comes from. So it is with those who engage in this so-called prayer. From whom they receive gifts is of little importance. They want the gifts, but not the Giver.

Now we understand what James says, "Ye ask, and receive not." Such prayer will never be answered. Would the great giver separate the gift from Himself? Then God would not be God. This doesn't mean that the request is never granted. It is quite possible that blessings seem to be given and are accepted as an answer to prayer. But that makes the matter even worse, for God sometimes gives things with His left hand—giving in judgment and not in His favor.

31

Those who pray to a god of their own making for a gift are still with us. They have never learned to love the true God. Therefore they do not love their neighbor either. They say: "Go to and be warmed." These "masters" think they know everything and sit as kings on their thrones, judging others. They think that their prayers produce a sweet-smelling savor of incense to God. They need to understand the words of James: "Let every man be swift to hear, slow to speak." Grace teaches us to listen and become aware of our ignorance. In the closet God can use only people who have learned to see their ignorance.

Then there are the fighters. Perhaps they fight for God's truth, but it is possible to be zealous for the law in a carnal way. Even when men think they are fighting for God's truth, they can stand in His way. The worst thing is that when one prays this way he can imagine that he is experiencing God's nearness. The devil goes with him into the closet as an angel of light. One actually may be concerned with selfish desires and not even be aware of it. If man were really conscious of his evil desires he would not dare come to God in that condition. That is why we need the uncovering work of the Spirit. Our first prayer therefore should be: "Lord, uncover me to myself."

I can even ask for conversion, for protection, for salvation, for heaven, and yet pray amiss. For instance, I can pray for conversion without desiring conversion. I can ask to be saved without grieving over my own lostness. I can ask for salvation but not acknowledge my sin. I can ask for heaven and yet not want the God of heaven. I can pray for everything that God's children possess and yet be content to be without the Lord Himself.

Is there still anyone who thinks he can pray? I hope not! He deceives himself if he thinks so. I can understand it if someone now says, "If that is how it is, then I might as well stop praying, because I can pray only improperly and that is an abomination to God." Such a reaction is quite understandable. God's Word doesn't mean here that we ought to stop praying. They who pray improperly are not rejected because they ask too much of the Lord. They do not ask enough! The problem is that they ask for things that gratify their own ego. A true prayer is first of all concerned with God and His cause and then with your neighbor's. Such a prayer always brings benefits for yourself, for when you are concerned about the Lord's cause, you also experience a blessing for your own heart.

We cannot be at the throne of grace too often; we can never ask too much of the Lord, only too little. Therefore do not stop, do not give up! Satan also comes at this time and says, "You cannot pray, your prayer is only sinful in God's eyes and the best thing is to stop." Satan uses every means to keep you from praying in secret in the closet. Therefore the first thing to pray is, "Lord, teach us to pray"—a prayer for a prayer. At the same time pray, "Lord, teach me to die to my lusts, to my pride, to my self-esteem."

There is one prayer that has never been rejected—that is, "O God be merciful to me, a sinner." That prayer can never be prayed too often. Here a sinner never asks too much; such a prayer is not improper.

One can tell when God's people have been in the closet. There they have so deeply bowed down before God that they lost all the weapons of war and rebellion. There "many masters" have lost their mastership. There they have also died to their lusts. They have become people whom God can use and who can mean something to others.

What we therefore need is the Spirit of prayer who is able to cleanse our lustful hearts and is willing to sanctify our prayers.

4

Arrogant

"The Pharisee stood and prayed thus with himself, God, I thank thee, that I am not as other men are, extortioners, unjust, adulterers, or even as this publican. I fast twice in the week, I give tithes of all that I possess" (Luke 18:11-12).

For several hundred years before the birth of Christ times were very dark in Israel. The people had forgotten the commandments of the Lord, and where God's precepts are not honored, true prayer does not exist either.

Fortunately there were people who were grieved because of this and who zealously sought to show the old paths to the people, while they themselves tried to walk in them as well. They were the Pharisees. The original intention of the Pharisees was therefore commendable. But when the best degenerates, it becomes the worst. The

Pharisees sought merit by walking the old paths. They no longer were indebted to God, but God was really indebted to them. So precise were they in their lives that the commandments given by God were not enough; many more stipulations had to be added. The scribes filled scores of books with ordinances that they thought up and the Pharisees practiced them as exactly as possible. It was therefore understandable that they self-righteously felt they were better than the multitude that did not know the law. Such Pharisees abused the precious Christ the most.

The same thing can still be seen today. Just like the Pharisees, there are those who have more commandments than the Lord has given in His perfect law. It is deadly dangerous when man becomes stricter than the lawgiver Himself. Such people crucify Christ anew every day.

In reality it is of course not true that they lived a more exact life than God prescribed in His holy law. This is evident in the prayer of the Pharisee. With all the extra law stipulations, the Pharisees looked for sin where it was not to be found. They sought sin in many things and forgot that sin is not present in many things, but only in man's evil heart. They overlooked their own sinful hearts while they were easily offended by many trivial matters. They did not strictly observe what the Lord had commanded in the first and great commandment, "Thou shalt love the Lord thy God above all and thy neighbor as thyself."

But why should we keep on talking about others? In this way we cover up for ourselves. We need to see ourselves in the Pharisee's prayer so that our pride may be uncovered and we will be so ashamed before God that we end up in the closet of the publican!

There stands the Pharisee, praying in the temple, in the presence of God. Or more accurately said, there he stands giving thanks, for he says, "O God, I thank thee." He begins with thanksgiving. Of course, in itself it is good to thank God. Scripture says, "In everything give thanks." We can never acknowledge the Lord enough for all His mercies. If we would take notice of the fact that we do not stop sinning and God does not stop doing good to us, we would have much more cause for thanksgiving than we can ever know. Where this acknowledgment is lacking in our prayer, very much is lacking. True thankfulness always glorifies God.

But we should not start our prayers so mechanically and so glibly with "I thank thee." In the first place, by nature we are not such thankful creatures. We must say this to our shame. Secondly, we must be sure it isn't just custom or habit, lest we thank God for something we have never experienced as a need. I'm afraid that often thanksgiving is made for forgiveness of sin, while sin has never become a burden. Thanksgiving can be given for Jesus' blood without knowing experientially the preciousness of that blood.

In any case, the Pharisee does not have true thankfulness, because he thanks God that he is not like other men. There would be nothing wrong with this prayer if he had given thanks that he did not *act* as other men, such as thieves, adulterers, and the like, and he had only said, "O God, I thank Thee that I do not act as other men." We can never thank God enough that we are kept from an offensive life.

But the unfortunate thing with this man is that he thinks that he is not like such men. This shows that he doesn't know himself. He doesn't know that he, too, is full of unrighteousnesses, if not in deed, then certainly in words or thoughts. He doesn't know his sinful nature and what must a man do at the throne of grace when he doesn't know his sinful condition?

When it comes to sin this man is busy with others. People who don't know themselves are always busy with others. They don't seem to have any sins of their own to confess to God, but the sins of others are broadly proclaimed and vehemently condemned.

The Pharisee prayed to himself. People often talk to themselves and imagine they are praying to God. True prayer, however, involves waiting on God for His favor and grace, and listening to what the Lord says.

First the Pharisee says what he is not and then he begins to say what he is. "I fast twice in the week, I give tithes of all that I possess." This Pharisee does much more than the Lord required. If he were God, he would do things differently and better. Therefore Christ says of the Pharisees, "Ye lade men with burdens grievous to be borne." In the eyes of the Pharisee it was impossible for the multitude that did not know the law to be saved. How could those ordinary people pray? So high above the masses did the Pharisees place themselves that the common people actually thought that only Pharisees prayed rightly. The Pharisees kept ignorant people from entering their closets in prayer.

The Pharisee's prayer is now completed. He has nothing to ask, but presents a long list of good works to the Lord. He therefore feels that it would be fitting for God to thank him for everything he has done in His service.

We have called the Pharisee's prayer an arrogant prayer. Or isn't it arrogant for a man to dare draw near to his creator as if nothing happened in paradise? Man is a fallen creature, and that is terrible! But it is much worse when we ignore our fallen state and never bemoan the deep abyss that resulted. What an abomination this prayer must be in the eyes of a righteous God! This Pharisee mistook his pride for true piety. The Pharisees thought they served God. Paul, who also was a Pharisee, says that of himself. Paul thought he prayed well when he persecuted the church of God and he sincerely thought his prayer was pleasing to God.

Taken in context, Christ told this parable with an eye to those who trust in their own righteousness. Man can be sincere and yet deceive himself. Sin can be present in the most sacred activities. Today these words of Christ have no other message than that we may learn to see ourselves here. Ever since the prayer of the Pharisee has been known there are people who pray, "O God, I thank Thee that I am not as the Pharisee." But that also can be the prayer of a Pharisee, a prayer without self-knowledge, wherein one rests on the belief that one is not as bad as others.

The arrogant prayer of the Pharisee can reveal itself in different forms. It may even be that Pharisees pray the prayer of the publican. Self-knowledge is the first requirement for which we ought to pray. We will pray: "Lord, can a Pharisee still be converted?" Then we implore: "O God, be merciful to me a Pharisee." An almighty deed of God is necessary to arrest the publican on the path of sin. Can we therefore not say that a double measure of God's Spirit is necessary to break the Pharisee? They both live in us. But the Pharisee lives deep down within us and appears to be so godly and pious that we hardly discern him.

There is no more hopeless condition than having no awareness of sin. How shall we appear before the Lord with our own righteousness? Even our good works are filthy rags, says Scripture. They are no more than glittering sins, because in the final analysis, like the Pharisee, we still give honor to ourselves.

When the Pharisee names extortioners, unjust, adulterers, and publicans as sinners, he is referring to the second table of the law. But he is silent concerning the first table, which speaks about man's relationship with God. Even if you have crammed more laws into your head than God has given, everything in your life and prayers is lacking unless you have the relationship that the first table of the law requires. The Lord doesn't ask for many things; He asks only for love. He prefers to see a fallen Peter at His feet, who with bitter tears acknowledges that he has sinned against all the commandments, but who can call God as witness that he still loves Him.

When we have seen that we have sinned against the first great commandment, then we will see that we are guilty of transgressing all the other commandments. Then we become the extortioners, the unjust, the adulterers, and the publicans. Then we become what we are. Realizing this will give us the right attitude in our prayer to God. We can never bring too much guilt to the Lord. We never bring enough guilt to Him.

This parable is told not only as a warning, but also for our comfort. It is a comfort for those who have a burden of guilt, to encourage them not to stay away from God's throne because of their unworthiness. They do not place any value on their prayers because they know they are nothing in themselves. Yet such prayers do have value with God, as we will see in subsequent chapters.

You, child of God, who by grace have come to see that you cannot present the Lord with any virtues, cannot by yourself rise above the attitude of the Pharisee. For you especially there is the danger of ascribing merit to the fruits of your new life. If they become the ground of your standing before God and you build on your tears, your prayers, your experiences, and everything else that sprang from your choice of serving the Lord, the result is much darkness in your prayer life and great barrenness.

It is even worse when a child of God becomes puffed up by free grace, raises himself above others, bolts the door of the closet with locks of hardness and pride, and acts as if salvation is not as possible for others as it was for him. Here the Pharisee attitude has revived in a regenerated heart, and God cannot use His child. The church today is not free from this sin.

The knife of conviction must be used to cut men until they are free from pride and thus freed from self. Only death can bring complete freedom; on earth we will struggle with the Pharisee attitude. Remember this and let your prayer continually be, "O God, be merciful to me, a Pharisee."

5

Humble

"And the publican, standing afar off, would not lift up so much as his eyes unto heaven, but smote upon his breast, saying, God be merciful to me a sinner"   (Luke 18:13).

After the Israelites had been conquered by the Romans, it became necessary for them to pay taxes and customs to their oppressors. Publicans were wealthy, corrupt Israelites who promised to pay a given sum into the Roman treasury for each province in Israel. In order to obtain sufficient amounts to pay the taxes, to generously compensate for their own labor and risk, and often to pay Roman governors for allowing oppressive practices, the publicans excessively overcharged their fellow citizens. They kept large portions of the money they received to enrich themselves and live extravagantly. It was the publican Zacchaeus who admitted that he had obtained many goods by fraud (Luke 19).

Needless to say, the publican's riches led to a sinful life. Where there is plenty of money, the doors of sinful pleasures open up. The same loose principles that allowed their consciences to deceive their fellow citizens also allowed them to live in sin. The Bible often mentions "publicans and sinners" in the same breath.

No wonder that the Jews refused to associate with the publicans. They were traitors and oppressors of their own people and they were shameless and lawless men. They had made themselves worthy of the contempt of the people. A poor honest man would never accept charity from a publican. Seen in this light we can somewhat appreciate the Pharisee's prayer. Aren't we also, when we hear of the publicans, thankful we aren't like them? If Christ's mission had not been to save sinners, He would never have entered the custom house except to destroy the publicans in righteous indignation.

But here we see a publican, not at the receipt of customs, but in the temple, bowing down before God. God has become too strong for him and sin has become too much for him. The man looks for a place where he can pour out his heart before the Lord. Although he must acknowledge that it would be just if he were cast away from God's presence forever, he cannot stop seeking after God. One might suppose that such a person would flee as far away from God as possible, but no, he clings to the Lord; if he perishes, he perishes.

How the people who entered the outer court must have despised him! They must have shunned him as if he were a leper. The Pharisee is so indignant that he cannot refrain from mentioning the publican's appearance in his prayer. It took a lot of nerve for such a vile specimen of humanity to appear inside the temple!

But the one who had the least nerve was the publican. He knew better than anyone that he was the lowest creature, and with every step he took he knew too that he was unclean. He dared go no further; he stood afar off with downcast eyes. It would be a miracle for him if he would not perish there before God's holy countenance! His humility was not put on. Some people say very humbly that they are satisfied with the lowest place, but underneath this humility is pride. What a good thing it is to have an attitude of humility in prayer! Humility is the first thing a sinner learns and also the last thing.

With downcast eyes the publican smites his hand on his breast. When things go wrong people often hit themselves on the head to show that they don't know what to do. But when they see that the root of their problem is their own sin, they don't strike their head, but rather their breast, just as this publican did. The publican places his hand where his spiritual pain is: "Here it is, inside of me," he seems to say as he strikes his hand on his breast. And that is where the seat of sin is. This publican has been mortally wounded with the sword of his own sin.

Not until now does he begin to speak; the attitude of his heart preceded his words. What an immense difference there is in the way we draw near to God. We can come with the same words the publican used and yet lack his attitude of heart. Much more important than what we say is the attitude in which we approach the Lord. The all-knowing God looks at the heart first.

"O God, be merciful to me a sinner," the publican cried. The Greek actually says, "O God, be merciful to me *the* sinner." The publican feels himself to be not just *a* sinner, but *the* sinner. For him only one sinner exists and that is he.

As long as we are just *a* sinner, one among many, and as long as the concept of sinner is still a general idea for us, then we have not yet become *the* sinner before God. We can acknowledge that we are a sinner among many with faults and shortcomings, but never feel personal guilt. When we finally do feel guilt, we don't try to excuse ourselves by pointing to others, but we ourselves become the only and greatest sinner.

What does it actually mean to be a sinner before God? To understand that we will see what the original Greek says. There a word is used that means "missing the mark." We need to realize that we have missed the excellent mark for which

46

we were created in paradise—to live to God. We missed the mark because we broke away from God to live to self. The prophet Daniel named many of King Belshazzar's sins when the hand on the wall wrote "Weighed in the balances, and found wanting." But the chief sin of Belshazzar was that, "God in whose hand thy breath is, and whose are all thy ways, hast thou not glorified."

Let us meditate on these words, "missing the mark." We not only *have* sin, but we *are* sin. Man comes to God, not only with sin, but as one who is sin.

Doesn't that humble you? What else can you do but ask for grace? The publican offered no tithes and didn't boast of fasting twice a week. He could only ask for grace—grace or death.

When a sinner prays like that for grace he leaves God free to grant grace or withhold it. God's sovereignty is acknowledged and not a word is spoken against God, even if no answer comes from heaven. Grace leaves God free, otherwise it is not grace. It is hardly necessary to add that such a humble prayer has no value in the eyes of the one who prays. Sometimes the complaint is heard, "If my prayer were only a true prayer." Here the idea is that there is some merit in prayer itself. But if you are waiting for a good prayer you will wait in vain until you die.

The publican didn't and couldn't wait until he knew his prayer was true. Moreover, no prayer has ever been heard because of any intrinsic value of the prayer. Humility cannot move heaven. The publican knew that. Therefore he doesn't place any value on his humility. Had he done that, he would have something to offer to God and then, in principle, there would have been very little difference between him and the Pharisee.

Be sure you understand that the attitude of your heart cannot move God. If you think that, you will end up in the dark. Humility consists in being dependent on grace alone. Many prayers have not been answered because in His wisdom God has determined otherwise. Yet a prayer for grace has never been rejected. The publican experienced this, for he went to his house justified.

Does the answer always come so quickly? Grace is all-sufficient, whether a crumb falls from heaven for the first time, or whether something more is given later on. The lesson here is that ultimately there is only one thing we should pray for—grace. Has that become your prayer?

What a short prayer! But for the Lord it is not too brief, for a prayer for grace is always accompanied by a broken heart. To ask for grace includes the acknowledgment of God's righteous judgment and of our own lost condition. It means that we agree with God's justice and confirm our sentence, even if our request would be rejected.

This is very humiliating for man. Because the crown has fallen from his head he must sink and perish, except he end up in the arms of God's good pleasure—that is Christ. Christ is the only fountain of grace. He must do what we cannot do. To pray for grace is yielding oneself to the sovereignty of God and simultaneously resting in the mercy of God.

Such a prayer glorifies God. It is well-pleasing to the Lord when a fallen man acknowledges his fall before the holy throne. It is well-pleasing to the Lord when a prodigal son or daughter comes back in this way. Yes, the Lord waits for such a son or daughter. When they stood afar off and dared not raise their eyes, they could not see that there was a Savior who was waiting to pay their debt.

Doesn't this encourage you? The Lord is actually waiting to pay your debt. There is a Redeemer for the debts you owe and it is the Savior's joy to freely bestow His meritorious grace on publicans and sinners. We are never too wicked to come to Jesus. We can only be too good in our own eyes.

Do not despair then! Do not give up! It is Satan who keeps you away from the throne of grace, suggesting that you are too wicked, for Satan also knows that it is a throne of grace. He does not want you to end up in the arms of God's mercy, and therefore he seeks any means to keep you from the closet. To one he says, "You are good enough" and to another he says, "You are too wicked."

Because sin (remains in us until our last breath, we will never get beyond the publican's prayer. The closer we are drawn to God, the greater our sin seems to us. Before His throne, in His holy light, we always stand in need of more grace. Not only is grace experienced as a free gift, but it becomes a daily way of living in Christ. Otherwise we would perish. Therefore the last prayer to be prayed will be, "O God, be merciful to me a sinner," for only publicans and sinners are received at the gate of heaven.

6

Bold

"Let us therefore come boldly unto the throne of grace, that we may obtain mercy, and find grace to help in time of need" (Heb. 4:16).

Humble prayer does not exclude boldness. In our prayer life humility and boldness are not contradictions. The first is found by looking at self and the latter is found by looking to Christ.

Boldness is needed to appear at the throne of a king, a symbol of his power and majesty. But how much more boldness is needed to approach the throne of the King of kings! Who dares approach where even the angels cover their faces, as Isaiah saw in a vision and cried out, "Woe is me! for I am undone; because I am a man of unclean lips." We are not referring to the boldness of the Pharisee who without hesitation entered the temple of God. That is a false bold-

51

ness. We are addressing those who have seen their own vileness before the holiness of God and who, looking at their daily lives, ask themselves, "Isn't God getting weary of me?" They dare not approach and the more they see of God's holiness and majesty, the less boldness they have to approach the throne of grace.

The author of the Epistle to the Hebrews knows that this boldness cannot be found with the sinner. Yet he encourages sinners to come and enter. That is why he points to the ground of this boldness by using the word, "therefore." "Let us therefore come," he says. The basis for this word is found in the previous verses where Christ is portrayed as the great high priest who takes the sinner's side before the Father.

In the old covenant the high priest stood between God and man to atone for sin. The prophets also stood between the Lord and the people. The difference between prophet and priest was that the prophet stood on God's side to speak to man on behalf of God, whereas the high priest was on the side of man to speak to God on behalf of man—not so much to speak words, but with the sacrifice of atonement for sin. That is why the Epistle to the Hebrews so emphatically stresses that the high priest must in all things be like man, except having no sin, so that he could experience man's needs and be tempted by the same sins. Such a high priest is Christ. As He sits at the right hand of God on the throne in heaven, He is not only prophet to speak to man on God's behalf, but He is also priest to speak to God on behalf of man. He does not offer the sacrifices of bullocks and goats as Aaron and his sons did, but He Himself was the perfect sacrifice on the cross of Calvary. Christ was the sacrifice that God required to satisfy completely the guilt of sin. Not one high priest of the old covenant could offer this sacrifice. Even if the priests would have offered themselves, their blood could not pay, because they also were sinful people and God required a perfect sacrifice.

Therefore Christ had to become man to be the intercessor. He was conceived by the Holy Ghost and therefore was without sin. He was born of the virgin Mary; therefore He came into the misery of sin, under the same curse as mankind. In all points He, like man, was tempted, yet he did not sin. Christ knows the intensity and fury of temptation and He knows how strong sin is. Therefore He can have pity on the sinner who comes before His throne.

Christ is an interceding high priest who takes the side of a guilty sinner. As our divine advocate He doesn't condone sin as human lawyers sometimes do, but points the divine judge to the payment for sin.

"Let us therefore come boldly unto the throne of grace." This is strong encouragement for those who humbly pray. Humility and boldness can go together. All may come to the throne because of grace—a gift offered through Christ's death. Nowhere do we read that some may not come; and the Lord has never cast anyone away from His throne.

Satan tries to persuade sinners to keep away from the throne. "First you have to conquer sin; first you have to improve yourself," he says. If we would heed his voice, no sinner could ever draw near to God, because we cannot cleanse ourselves. Child of God, boldness isn't found in yourself or in your works or prayers. All your works cannot open the entrance to the throne of grace. There comes a time when God closes heaven to teach you that there is no approach to God without Christ, and you learn that your prayer is not worth anything unless the praying high priest makes intercession for you.

Not only Satan says that it is impossible to come to God's throne, but the sinner says so too. The more his own righteousnesses fall away, the less he dares draw near to the throne. God said He would accept us "When I see the blood," not "When I see you." There is nothing you can do to fix yourself up. Boldness can be found only in Christ. When we come in our own strength God is a consuming fire. When a sinner leans on Christ, he receives a boldness, a holy courage, that causes him to draw near to God. He who sits at the right hand of God and ever lives to make intercession for His people is the same One who also descended into the depths of man's fall.

The exalted Christ is very willing to be the way for those who admit they are sinners. When such do not dare draw near to the throne, Christ lets them know that in Him it is a throne of grace. Let humility then join with boldness. Let them take hold of the great high priest claiming these words: "Whosoever comes to me, I will in no wise cast out."

No one needs to be afraid that humility will suffer from boldness. The bolder one becomes in Christ, the more humble one becomes in himself. Otherwise it is not true boldness but evidence of spiritual pride, or at least a sign of insensitivity or coldness. This can occur even in the life of a believer.

Bold prayer glorifies Christ. He who learns to use Christ as the way and the door gives Him work to do. And the intercessor is glorified most through the work of intercession; for He has not come to be served, not even in prayer, but to serve, also in prayer. Bold prayer also glorifies God the Father. It is well-pleasing to God when sinners come to God through Christ, for the Father Himself has said: "This is my beloved Son in whom I am well pleased." If you do not see the Son, you will never see the Father. No less is the Holy Spirit glorified here. The same Spirit who clothes with humility also clothes with boldness. True boldness is not a matter of working ourselves up to a state where we feel ourselves worthy before God; the opposite is true.

In this light we take a closer look at the word *boldness* as it is found in the original Greek. Literally it means "not keeping anything back"; in other words, it means to confess everything. Keeping nothing back reminds us of a childlike attitude. Thus the rule for salvation and prayer is: "Except ye become as a little child." We understand that true boldness does not make little ones proud, but makes proud ones small. We descend to the depths of humility. That is why boldness is found in the valley of humility and these two go hand in hand.

Keeping nothing back and telling everything gets in the way of our pride. False shame covers our sins. How many unconfessed sins exist before the all-knowing God? How necessary is the continual, uncovering work of the Spirit! The psalmist understood this well when he prayed, "Cleanse thou me from secret faults."

Surely the lack of boldness reveals the lack of a childlike attitude. If we would lose our desire to grow in eminence, we would find more boldness in the valley of humility. Christ and the operation of His Spirit are found in its depths.

Such childlike boldness bears rich fruits. Our text says, "that we may obtain mercy, and find grace to help in time of need." Mercy is the inward compassion of God whereby He is moved in Christ. Grace is what a sinner receives in answer to and possibly during prayer. Mercy and grace are all-sufficient. One crumb of these is worth more than all the riches of the world. They make up for everything, even though the way may be difficult.

Let us for a moment meditate on the words "help in time of need." Those who pray as described above find help in God, not in themselves. "In time of need" is God's time. God's time is always the best time. The Lord never comes too early or too late. Often God's child says, "Now must be God's time." But the Lord sometimes lets us wait. And often we learn more during that time of waiting than when help is received. If all prayers were answered right away, God's people would conclude that it was because they prayed so well.

We have learned that there still is a throne of grace, a time during which no one can say that he may not come. God doesn't say anywhere that we may not come. However, we *do* read, "Thou wilt not come to me." Therefore, if you are a stranger to prayer, it is not because God has closed the entrance to His throne of grace. God still calls to you, "Turn ye to me and be ye saved." One day the throne of grace will become a throne of judgment and never again will there be grace to help in time of need. Remember that the throne of grace doesn't last forever. Let this call of God drive you to the throne of grace now!

7

True

"*Likewise the Spirit also helpeth our infirmities: for we know not what we should pray for as we ought: but the Spirit itself maketh intercession for us with groanings which cannot be uttered. And he that searcheth the hearts knoweth what is the mind of the Spirit, because he maketh intercession for the saints according to the will of God*" (Rom. 8:26, 27).

In prayer it isn't only important how we pray, but we must also ask the question: "What shall we pray for?" From our text it is evident that we cannot give an answer to this question. "For," says the apostle Paul, "we know not what we should pray for as we ought."

Sometimes we assume that we are able to pray well. This holy and tender activity is taught by heaven, but that doesn't mean God's people possess the ability to pray well. If anyone thinks he has mastered the art of prayer because he can testify to many answered prayers, he is an abomination before the Lord and an idolator before men.

The Bible saints did not know what they should pray for. The great Moses did not know what he should pray for when he asked to enter Canaan. Elijah, of whom we read that the prayer of the righteous availeth much, did not know what he was praying for when he asked, "O Lord, take away my life." The disciples knew just as little when they wanted to ask for fire from heaven to come upon the Samaritans. Neither did Paul know what to pray for when he pleaded with the Lord three times to have the thorn in his flesh removed. He didn't know that he needed the thorn.

It is a good thing that not all prayers are answered positively. Imagine if God would grant everything which men would request of Him! The fulfillment of our requests could easily become a judgment. The Israelites received a king according to their wishes, but king Saul went from bad to worse. You see, we do not know what we should pray for as we ought. With our so-called knowledge and wisdom we only stand in the way of the Lord and ourselves.

How shall we pray? And what should we pray for? Certainly, above everything else a humble prayer should include the request for

God's grace. But in addition to God's grace we need to pray about temporary and eternal matters.

From God's Word we learn that two intercessors are needed in prayer: a pleading Christ because it is only for His sake that God the Father hears us, and also a purifying intercessor through whom our prayers are cleansed—the Holy Spirit, who, in Scripture is called the Spirit of supplication. Christ prays for His people and the Holy Spirit prays within His people as the Spirit of supplication, as a helper—"The Spirit helpeth our infirmities."

This means that a child of God is in himself not able to send up a sweet-smelling sacrifice of prayer that is acceptable to heaven. He is too infirm and powerless because of the impotence of sin, the impotence of foolishness, ignorance, and shortsightedness. He needs a helper. The meaning of "also helpeth" is literally "helping in our stead."

We need an illustration to understand what this means. Take, for example, a captain who hands the helm of his boat over to his young son who has to learn to guide the boat. It soon becomes apparent that it is better that the father stays close by, for with just the boy at the helm the boat will not stay on the right course; it will end up on the sandbanks, the rocks, or in the swift current. Now what does the father do? He doesn't shove the boy aside and say, "Let go of the wheel!" No, the father does what it says in the original of our text: he helps in his stead. Together the father and his son stand at the helm. If danger threatens, the hands of the father are strong enough to turn the helm so that the boy's hands turn with the father's. Yet the father does more than help. In actual fact it is not the boy, but his father who keeps the boat on course. That illustrates what Scripture means when it says that the Spirit of God "also helpeth our infirmities" in prayer.

Failures, including failure in prayer, are due to sin. For example, there are sandbanks of self-love, rocks of carnal desires, and swift currents of spiritual pride. All these conditions prevent prayer from ascending as a sweet-smelling sacrifice to God. So what does the Spirit of supplication do? The Spirit doesn't thrust us away from the closet and say, "Forget about praying; you cannot pray." No! That is what Satan says. Instead, the Spirit of the Lord comes to help us with sighs and groanings which cannot be uttered. He stoops down to our needs, like the father stood by his boy, helping him to do what he couldn't do by himself.

"The Spirit Himself maketh intercession for us with groanings which cannot be uttered." Our deepest needs are the most difficult to express in words. A child of God has times when he cannot explain himself to the Lord; he cannot find the words to describe his condition; his needs and joys are deeper than words can express. What are words? Often they are just sounds. Often words serve to cover up our ignorance and lack of understanding, and consequently our fellow man, even our closest friend cannot understand what our words are trying to convey. Well, then, who can therefore find the right words to explain himself to God? It seems the deeper the experience, the more powerless we feel to explain these feelings to the Lord.

Of course, it is true the more childlike we are, the better. And it is a child who stammers most. The more God's people become like children, the more they need a helper, just as a child stumbling over words to explain an event looks to his mother as if to say, "Mother, you help me with the right words." So it is with the intercessory work of the Spirit of supplication, who with wordless groanings helps put the concerns of God's child before God's throne because His child cannot find the words to express himself. God's dear Spirit descends into the heart and performs a purifying work in the prayer of a helpless child who cannot pray as he ought. We can therefore speak of true prayer only when the work of this perfect intercessor is present.

When we keep in mind the words "helping in our stead," we see that the Spirit not only helps, but also takes our place. These two meanings cannot be separated, for intercession is also necessary in prayer. First, there can be times of barrenness in our prayer life when the outward form of prayer is present, but the activity of the heart is absent. Yet there still lives a cry of the new life, for that new life cannot perish. When David kept silent in his state of prayerlessness, he says that his bones waxed old through his roaring all the day long. That is the crying to God of the new life worked by the Holy Spirit. The Spirit's intercessory work in prayer goes on during times of prayerlessness. The new life of regeneration cannot be at rest when there is outward coldness. God's Spirit groans for us even though the heart remains without desire. Then the new life of God's Spirit prays instead of the cold heart.

Helping in our stead also means that the Holy Spirit sometimes turns the helm of prayer so that the groanings of the Spirit contend against the desires of the one who is praying. We should keep in mind that often we do not know what we should pray for. When, for example, Paul prays to have the thorn in his flesh taken away, the groanings of the Spirit go against the groanings of Paul. Three times Paul repeats this prayer: "Take it away." But the Spirit prays against him: "Let him keep it, for he needs the thorn to keep him from pride."

A child of God may pray for things he sincerely thinks he needs, saying, "Lord, please give it to me." But the Spirit prays, "Give him not." It is possible to pray for precious things, but the Spirit says, "Take it away." What a painful matter it is when the Spirit prays in opposition to the flesh.

God's Spirit doesn't do this to aggravate us. It is for our well-being if the helm is turned around. God's Spirit prepares us for eternity and does only that which is good. Blessed we are if we can rest in this. Then the Spirit sanctifies our grief and the love of God is experienced too.

"And He that searcheth the heart," says verse 27, "knoweth what is the mind of the Spirit, because He maketh intercession for the saints according to the will of God." God the Father knows the heart. What is the heart without the sanctifying influences of the Holy Spirit when the all-knowing God searches it? When God's Spirit takes up His abode in our hearts we are changed, because "He maketh intercession for the saints according to the will of God." This means that the Spirit prays in accordance with God's will and cleanses the prayers of the saints in order that God can be pleased with them.

Blessed are you if you often experience your failures, for there is work for the Spirit. The more the Spirit works, the more you learn to pray according to the will of God, the more trust, peace, and divine instruction you will receive. When we think we can pray well, we deceive ourselves in this most holy work and there is less work for the Spirit to do.

We next turn to the Holy Spirit's work of sanctification, that is, the continuous renewal of the heart, which is absolutely necessary. It is also a continual uncovering of the abysses of our sinful hearts, so that we are more and more cut off from ourselves and turned to God to be renewed in the image of Christ. Christ is always concerned with God's glory and never His own. That is also the work of the Spirit: to point to Christ. Again and again our prayers must end in Him. Here it is experienced: "He that abideth in me, and I in him, the same bringeth forth much fruit: for without me ye can do nothing."

Whatsoever is born of the flesh is flesh. Thanks be to God that the Spirit prays against the flesh, for otherwise we would be lost forever. What is born of the Spirit is spirit. Man's renewed spirit learns to will what God wills. God's Spirit teaches us to pray to be set free from this body of sin. We are taught to pray with the Spirit and against our own flesh.

This is not a longing for death; death is not to be longed for. We long to be delivered from sin and to worship God forever. This is exemplified in the prayer in the last book of the Bible: "And the Spirit and the bride say: Come." Not the bride, but the Spirit is mentioned first, because the Spirit has prayed this prayer for the bride. This prayer will be answered and the bridegroom will come!

8

Pleading

"Hitherto have ye asked nothing in my name: ask, and ye shall receive, that your joy may be full" (John 16:24).

In this chapter of John we have the Lord's farewell address. Soon the members of the Sanhedrin will come to take Him to Pilate's judgment seat. Then the disciples will be alone and feel deserted because their Jesus, on whom they had set all their hope, will be gone. To whom can they go for the words of eternal life? To lose Him is to lose all.

But Christ, who is departing from them, knows this even better than they realize. He knows His own and He knows how poor and miserable they are without Him. That is why His thoughts turn to them even before they will feel His absence.

The fleshly ties must be broken. "It is expedient for you that I go away." Christ must die; there is no other way. Only through His death can He bring His church to life. Even afterwards He cannot stay on earth, because He must ascend to prepare a place for His children. Now, while He faces His dreadful death and descent into hell, He still remembers His disciples. He doesn't leave His disciples alone. He leaves them everything they need: His name.

What is in a name? The most beautiful human names can cover the worst deeds. Samson had a beautiful name meaning child of the sun; but how dark was the end of this child of the sun. The name of Jesus Christ, the Lord, however, is not merely a name; it is an expression of who He is for His own. His name is the only ground for prayer, the only pleading ground when there is nothing left to plead on. Even if a penitent sinner prays day and night, God cannot accept his prayer except in the name of Christ. Even the most humble prayer cannot be accepted, for there is not one sinner who can plead on his own merits.

In the school of prayer much instruction is found in the words of Christ: "Hitherto have ye asked nothing in my name." Certainly, the disciples had prayed. They were not strangers to prayer. But they had prayed to God without reference to the name of Christ. They lacked a foundation for their prayers. Even after three years of intimate acquaintance with Christ they still knew so little of His person. They had learned to know Jesus through His benefits, and they were not without true love for Him. Their love was so deep that they were willing to sacrifice their lives for Him. Not only Peter, but also other disciples had voiced their willingness to die for Him (and they meant it), even though they did not realize what they were saying.

True love is the test. God is love, and we do not have true love unless Christ is in us and we are in Him. Our guide on love is found in I Corinthians 13.

But love must be accompanied by knowledge. The disciples had much love for the person of Christ but they had little knowledge or understanding of His mission. Near the time of His death, the Lord said, "Have I been so long with you, and yet hast thou not known me, Philip?" If Christ had asked His disciples what had to be done for the salvation of souls, then all would have been lost, because they tried to keep Him from death. They were much more concerned about what they had to do for Him than what He had to do for them. They had no eye for His suretyship; they didn't think that was necessary. They had already been dividing the positions in the kingdom of heaven among themselves and had argued over who would be the greatest. The thought of a dying king was beyond their understanding.

Therefore they had not considered using His name as a pleading ground before God. They had not prayed in Jesus' name, because they were not aware that God's justice must still be satisfied. When they were dividing the kingdom and striving to be the greatest, they assumed they were sure of their standing in the kingdom. But the time would soon come when they will all forsake Him in spite of their love. They were going to realize that they have no special merit and their only hope for salvation lies in the name of a suffering and dying surety. "Afterwards," says Christ, "shall ye understand these things." And they understood later when the apostle said, "We love him, for he first loved us."

Once the disciples asked Christ, "Teach us to pray." They did not realize yet that the price of true prayer would be to lose their own good name. When divine instruction is given, many things have to be unlearned, even though the love of God has already been shed abroad in the heart. We must lose ourselves; we cannot rest in our conversion, good works, tears, prayers, or anything outside of Christ. Yes, that hurts, because we love to have something with which we can appear before God, a reputation with His people and with all men. We like to be called converted, humble people who know how to pray. Alas, we must acknowledge with shame that we, along with the disciples, strive for the greatest position.

It is necessary for God's Spirit to sever the communion experienced in prayer to teach His disciple that he lacks the ground of prayer. In this way he is taught to plead only on the merits of Christ, for only His merits have acceptance with God. Christ gives His people a ground outside of themselves, a pleading ground to which they may appeal, so that their prayers may find acceptance at the throne of God. This is a sure foundation. The loss of self is a happy loss; God's Spirit breaks down our pride and self-esteem in order to build us up in Christ. Thus He enables men to lay hold of Christ in His own work.

It is only in Christ that God the Father has revealed Himself as Jehovah, "I am that I am." He is the unchangeable, faithful God for unfaithful ones who have a thousand times forfeited their portion. The name of Jehovah expresses that the cause of the church is God's cause. When everything was hopeless in the valley of Achor, Joshua could say, "What wilt thou do unto thy great name?" It was as though he wanted to say, "Lord, it is Thy cause and Thy work."

To reveal Himself as Jehovah cost the Father the life of His Son. Behind the name *Jehovah* lies the name of *Jesus*. God is faithful to His people because Christ was cast away from Him. The Lord takes hold of His people because He let go of His Son. Christ was deserted by God so that deserters would have a ground to plead on.

Have you found that pleading ground? Or do you still pray without His name? Then your prayers lack a mediator. It is possible to have blessed experiences and taste divine comforts, but do we realize who has merited these experiences and comforts for us?

Man must be humbled and Christ's name exalted. There is no greater joy than to experience the "nevertheless" of faith. Christ says here, "that your joy may be full." If the anchor of prayer is cast inside the ship, there is no cause for joy. Such a ship must perish, even if the anchor is cast. This happens whenever the pleading ground is only in the form of tears, prayers, experiences, and emotions. These are indispensable components, of course, but are not the foundation of joy. The anchor of prayer must be cast outside the ship. Scripture speaks of "an anchor of the soul, both sure and steadfast, and which entereth into that within the veil, whither the forerunner is for us entered, even Jesus (Heb. 6:19, 20).

What a pleading ground we have "within the veil"! That is the heavenly sanctuary where Christ prays for His people. Salvation is anchored so high and so secure that no one can take it away. Even the devil's hands cannot reach there. The Lord takes care of His own work. Therein lies the fulness of joy! His is an eternal foundation and therefore our joy never ends.

Before Christ left His disciples He said: "In the world ye shall have tribulation." The storms will not cease. So severe will they be that God's child fears that he will yet perish. The billows of life continue to churn. But if our anchor is cast in that sure foundation, the ship will not smash on the rocks. Then there is joy even in tribulation. To the extent that the waves try with their might to pry the anchor loose, to that extent it becomes more deeply fastened. The storms can only cause a deeper union with God and a firmer hold on that name. The storms serve to make the anchor more secure and the link of prayer draws closer to the foundation. God uses these means to draw His child closer to Himself.

No one needs to be timid, fearing that he pleads on the name of Christ too soon. It is possible to do so too late, but never too soon. Some religious "experts" demand that a certain stage of spiritual knowledge must be reached before this pleading ground may be used. Alas, dead orthodoxy always keeps a sinner away from Christ. Certainly, there are preparatory ways which lead to the name of Christ. But these are detours made by man himself.

Whoever prays in Christ's name will surely be accepted. It is "for Christ's sake" that we receive what we receive. Here we have the ground of prayer on which eternal joy is founded.

9

Effectual

"The effectual fervent prayer of a righteous man availeth much" (James 5:16b).

When we consider effectual fervent prayer it is necessary that we are regulated by God's Word to keep us from fanaticism and a one-sided emphasis on these words of Scripture. Otherwise much harm can occur in our prayer life. Faith healers and charismatics appeal to this text and they look back with nostalgia to the apostolic age when so many miracles were performed. We must admit with sorrow that we do not look back with enough longing to that age. Much effectual fervent prayer was then offered. Great hope, faith, and love were then exercised. By comparison the church of today is barren and dead. Where are the mighty operations of the Holy Spirit in our time?

Yet, although we must agree with the charismatics that the state of the church leaves much to be desired, we simply cannot bring back the day of Pentecost with its outward signs of the Spirit. First of all, we should realize that the outpouring of the Holy Spirit was a unique and unrepeatable event. Pentecost represents the last of God's saving acts in the history of redemption. From God's side everything that had to be done was done. Just as in their once-for-all concrete form the events of Christmas, Good Friday, and Easter are not repeatable, so the once-for-all historical event of Pentecost will not be repeated.

To be sure, it must become Pentecost for us personally. We should not merely assume that because the Spirit has been poured out, we therefore possess that Spirit. We must personally experience the seeking love of the Spirit and be led by Him to newness of life. Yet, whoever looks for the same signs of wind and tongues of fire and languages will be disappointed. The Spirit was poured out at Pentecost, and we are not to be concerned with the outward signs anymore, but with the essential matters signified by the signs. Those who are preoccupied with the outward manifestations of the Spirit are actually trying to create a new Bible and are putting themselves on the same level as the inspired apostles through whom the miraculous powers were manifested in such a special way. We should realize that the special revelation of God, His Word, is a completed canon.

These introductory remarks have direct reference to the miracles of faith healing. These and other miracles of the apostolic age speak of a very special gift which came by way of laying on of hands and other means, whereby the apostles even raised the dead to life. They were the after-signs of Pentecost. Later on we do not hear of such powers. History has proved that the saving revelation of God—the Holy Scripture—was completed with the miracles of Pentecost. The church has accepted and understood this by faith. There is abundant proof that it did not look for a continuation of these past visible signs of God's special revelation.

To test the belief of those who say that we must possess the charismatic gifts of the apostolic age we should ask them this question: "Why can't you also raise the dead by your prayers? That happened too during the apostolic age!" Moreover, it is possible to become so fascinated by the miraculous gifts of the Spirit, that the regenerating work of the Spirit is neglected. Also, miracles are certainly no guarantee of true faith. Just think of the ten lepers. The nine also went to the priest to be declared healed by Jesus' words. They believed too. But of only one it is said that he had saving faith. It is possible to believe in miracles and yet have no knowledge of the regenerating power of the Spirit.

Effectual fervent prayer does not force God to give in to our needs or desires. We do not believe that sickness constitutes a lack of faith. Sickness may be a blessing. We should always distinguish between God's power and His will. Very often the Lord does not will for us what He can do for us. Even the apostle Paul experienced this when he had to leave his helper Trophimus sick. Such an incident certainly doesn't mean that there is lack of faith in the power of almighty God.

Therefore, let there be no doubt of the truth and power of the words of our text for all ages. The manifestation of the signs has changed, but God has not changed. He still performs His will through prayer. It is necessary to emphasize this because there are those who believe that James means that the prayer of the righteous avails much, but not all. They think "much" doesn't mean everything. The context, however, plainly indicates that the word *much* is used to show that true prayer is infinitely effectual. The emphasis is on the wonderful effectiveness of prayer.

Some limit effectual fervent prayer to great men of God like Elijah, about whom James is speaking in this chapter. Elijah possessed a unique power of prayer. "But I am no Elijah," these people will quickly add. Thank God that a powerful prayer does not depend on the power of the one who prays! No, effectual prayer is not a fruit of man; it is a gift from God that rises to heaven and which is inwardly experienced by man. This type of prayer arises with such fervency that there is no doubt that God will undertake for us. During or after prayer it is felt and believed that there is an effectual passage to heaven. There is a strong hope that this prayer will be answered.

Often there are attacks of doubt whether it was truly an effectual prayer, especially when the time of fulfillment tarries. Elijah saw a cloud the size of a man's hand only after he had prayed seven times. We learn from this that persevering prayer is a form of effectual prayer.

An effectual prayer is a power which excludes flesh and blood, because the power of the Spirit never pleases flesh and blood, in spite of man's attempts. Man must exclude himself. This means that personal interests recede to the background. According to the context, the subject of this effectual fervent prayer is intercession. Intercessory prayer is always prayer for someone else. Of course, this doesn't mean that a prayer for personal needs may not be included in effectual prayer. The Lord has said in His Word: "By prayer and supplication with thanksgiving let your requests be made known unto God." But let us always remember that true prayer makes us die to our self-interests. Effectual fervent prayer is always performed in weakness. The words of Paul, "When I am weak, then I am strong," apply here.

In this light we must understand the word *righteous*. Without righteousness prayer would be ineffectual. Righteous means to be in the right relationship to the Lord, so that the cause which brings us to the Lord is a right cause in His eyes. This will lead us to test ourselves. We must answer the question: What is my relationship to the Lord, and what are the self-interests of my request? To do this we need the convicting operation of God's Spirit.

The righteous are not people who are better than others. Except as God looks on them in favor, they have nothing. It was so with Elijah, Moses, and Paul, as we have seen. Effectual fervent prayer, therefore is a gift and it always will be a gift—even for the righteous. What a comfort this is for those who have no power in themselves! The word *righteous* certainly does not refer to a quality of man. The righteous are those who are clothed with grace. Therefore no one is too weak or too unworthy to lay his need or the needs of others before God. Only the opposite is true.

It is therefore wrong to say, "That is only for an Elijah." When James points to the effectiveness of prayer, he doesn't limit this to Elijahs; he takes that great Elijah as an example and adds that he was an ordinary man, "subject to like passions as we are."

It is of utmost importance that we don't think God is too small to meet our needs. It is possible to expect too little from God, but never too much. The sins of unbelief, of mistrust, and of seeking help outside of God make prayer ineffectual. *All* things are possible for those who believe.

Is it then true that it is our lack of faith that keeps us from being healed when we are sick? Here the questions begin to multiply. One could possibly come to the fearful conclusion: "If I could pray effectually I wouldn't be laid up with this sickness and I wouldn't have to carry this cross." But don't forget that there are more and greater things to be looked for. One man, seriously ill in a hospital, had something better and greater than healing to pray for. His only request was that the Lord might be glorified by his cross. He greatly desired to be healed, but he had an even greater desire to have the Lord as his portion forever. His prayer was answered. A miracle took place, not physically, but spiritually. His was an effectual prayer.

Be still then if you notice that your prayers for the removal or obtaining of a matter do not find acceptance. It is a sign that the Lord intends to lead you in a different way. But that shouldn't stop you from praying; a prayer for strength may be an equally effectual prayer. It is not so important *that* we suffer, but *how* we suffer. The results of such an effectual fervent prayer are better and greater than the removal of a cross. Isn't prayer effectual when the Lord gives grace in suffering? Isn't it an effectual prayer when one keeps standing in the midst of temptations against the onslaught of many enemies?

Effectual prayer doesn't have to be accompanied by outward power. It often bears fruit in secret. And aren't there many secret temptations and needs for which we need effectual prayer? Nothing is too insignificant to be worthy of effectual fervent prayer. Such prayer need not go beyond ordinary everyday matters. Is anything too insignificant for the Lord? God is glorified by the small and the weak.

Maybe the reason we lack much effectual fervent prayer is that we aim too high. We seek the special, the extraordinary, the sensational. We think that we have to increase, whereas we should decrease. The church has to realize that the kingdom of God is more than outward signs. Seen in this light, the smallest token of God's grace in answer to a sinner's prayer becomes as great as the miracle of rain from heaven for which Elijah prayed at Carmel. As we learn to live by the miracle of grace, prayer will avail much, and we will know that there is no greater power on earth than the power of effectual fervent prayer, for it is laying hold on the power of God.

10

Thankful

"In everything give thanks: for this is the will of God in Christ Jesus concerning you" (I Thess. 5:18).

The expression "thankful prayer" may sound strange. Prayer and thankfulness, however, always go together, not only because answered prayer requires thankfulness, but because we must acknowledge God's mercy toward unworthy sinners.

Thanksgiving in prayer is often a mere formality. Some people always begin prayer with a jubilant note of thanksgiving, but one wonders whether they really are so thankful. Do they know what they are thankful for? Thankfulness without a knowledge of personal salvation means that we are spiritually dead.

Is it possible to be thankful before you have received anything? No, that is impossible. But God's dealings with everyone of us are so gracious that every day we receive much to be thankful for. The Lord doesn't treat us according to our sins and thus we have abundant reasons for thankfulness. Even in a drop of water and a crumb of bread we ought to taste the Lord's grace, because we do not deserve anything.

Often we put thankfulness beyond our reach. Many people think that they must reach a high degree of progress in their prayer life before they can be thankful. But in our text the apostle Paul doesn't even ask whether the Thessalonians have any previous experience of answered prayer or how deeply led they are at this stage. He doesn't even ask if the Thessalonians are believers. He only points to the obligation of thanksgiving and says that it is the will of God that we thank Him in everything.

Whether or not we can point to answered prayers, we owe God thankfulness. Every day we receive much for which we didn't even ask. Even if we cannot point to any specific answers to prayer, we have reason to acknowledge the Lord for everything we are and have.

The apostle Paul wrote to the Romans: "Or despisest thou the riches of his goodness and forbearance and longsuffering, not knowing that the goodness of God leadeth thee to repentance?" Here we are reminded that there is more than

enough to be thankful for. If we would only rec-
ognize that everything we receive more than death
is grace. Some people have an outward form of
joy without an awareness of their sin, and others
forget that they owe the Lord thankfulness because of His goodness. The goodness of the Lord
ought to break and humble us, and turn us to
Him.

Even if God would withhold all answers to
prayer, He still is worthy to receive our thanksgiving for all the undeserved blessings He gives.
People who see this will have a high regard for
God, even if they have doubts about their own
salvation. Thankfulness begins with a broken and
contrite heart.

People who pray only to be relieved of their
troubles, pray to a god who exists merely to save
them from their troubles. But true prayer consists in wanting God even when He isn't needed
for relief from troubles. In other words, it is good
that troubles drive us to God, but His goodness
ought also to bring us to Him. When we need
God because of troubles, prayer can be mere self-
ishness. We see this in the example of the ten
lepers. Only one leper came back to give thanks.
The other nine went home and forgot who healed
them. They were happy with their healing. Joy
is not thankfulness; joy stays on a horizontal level,
but thankfulness rises from the depths. Joy is tied
to the blessings, but thankfulness binds us to the
giver of the blessings.

The word *thank* is related to the word *think*. Without thinking there is no thanking. We must think about our naked state and realize that everything we possess more than we had at birth is undeserved mercy.

Maybe there is someone who says that material blessings are not yet eternal blessings and that thankfulness for blessings received is only part of common grace and not of saving grace. But how else do we come to see ourselves as sinners who have no rights before God? Let us therefore begin at the point of thankfulness. The goodness of God, of which Paul speaks, and which we have just described, also is the means by which God's people are led to daily conversion. True thankfulness is born out of realization that we have no rights. This is true in small as well as great things, and in material as well as in spiritual matters.

Scripture says, "Forget not all his benefits." How forgetful sin has made us! Most of us are better at counting our troubles than our blessings. "In everything give thanks." We must return to God with thanks for all our undeserved blessings like the one leper who came to Christ when he was healed. "This is the will of God," says Paul. God justly demands our thankfulness. May Christ not ask: "Where are the nine?" Even though we have forgotten our blessings, the Lord has not forgotten; and therefore one day we will have to give an account of our stewardship. We must acknowledge that God is not unrighteous in demanding something which we cannot give Him by nature.

Do we know from experience what this inability is? We need the Lord to help us be thankful. God will teach an unthankful creature to be thankful, as He hears his prayer. If there is someone who complains that he cannot thank God as he ought, that complaint is known to God, and a broken and contrite heart He has never despised.

True thankfulness begins by recognizing our weakness. It ends in praising God, glorifying His Name, and praising His attributes in love. A mark of true thankfulness is that we love the giver more than the gifts. When God's creatures return to Him, there in His presence His goodness is experienced.

If we possess this love we always have something to be thankful for. If we are poor, we can be thankful for health. If we are sick, we can be thankful for the care we receive. If we have a cross, we can be thankful for what we still have.

"In everything give thanks." In everything? Yes, in everything—even in adversity. How is that possible? Paul understood this seeming impossibility when he was in prison with Silas and had his feet bound in stocks and his back cut open by the lashes he had received. He sang praises to God in the night. Paul knew that it is better to have adversity with God's presence, than prosperity without God's presence.

Thankfulness in adversity doesn't mean that we are indifferent to our suffering, that we don't feel our grief and have no sorrow. Thankfulness does not wipe out grief; that would be unnatural. But in sorrow God's sufficiency is felt and therefore, where there is grief, there may also be joy. Here the words of Revelation are applicable: "Here is the patience and the faith of the saints."

Patience means to endure willingly—like someone who carries a burden on his back and doesn't try to shake it off. He remains under the burden that God laid on him in His wisdom, to the glory of Christ's name. This situation is always for the well-being of the child of God, for he would rather bow under the cross than be without the cross and lose God.

The deepest trials often produce the greatest gratitude. The soul knows that these are God's personal dealings with him and that in this way the gold is purified because it is gold, and the grain is sifted because it is grain. When a gardener prunes the trees, he cuts off the branches that the sun cannot reach. The Lord cuts too, so that the sun of righteousness can enter. There is a reason for thankfulness, despite the pain of the pruning knife. When Jacob said, "All these things are against me," he should have said, "All these things are for me," because God was at work taking care of him. Blessed are they who believe without seeing. They shall glorify God, even though they don't know what the outcome will be. How sad that a child of God, like Jacob, is troubled by blind mistrust more frequently than he enjoys exercising faith in the unseen.

"In everything give thanks; for this is the will of God in Christ Jesus concerning you." "In Christ Jesus"—because of Him the Scriptures say; "Thanks be unto God for his unspeakable gift" (II Cor. 9:15). Thankfulness is to be found only in Christ. He is the gift and everything else is but a bonus. Just as in the school of prayer Christ must become known as the only pleading ground for prayer, so also in the school of thankfulness Christ must be known as the only ground for thankfulness. That is why God's Spirit gives us times when there is more reason for complaining than for thankfulness.

"This is the will of God in Christ concerning you." From man's point of view, Christ Jesus, in His substitutionary work had nothing to be thankful for. He only had reason to complain. On the cross He lost everything. He hung there naked, as poor as when He was born. He looked on while soldiers gambled for His clothing. Not only did He lose all His gifts; He also lost the giver. But He didn't cry about His condition, only that God had forsaken Him. Christ cried to God, but for Him there was no mercy; He had to bear the curse; He had no rights. The giver had turned against Him.

Christ suffered this way so that those who had no rights could live out of Him. We can never acknowledge enough that all blessings, material and spiritual, are given us only because of Christ. Our only ground for thankfulness lies therefore in Him. This ought to humble us and cause us to magnify the Savior. This is true thankfulness: to magnify the Lord out of a knowledge of our unworthiness.

11

Unfulfilled

"And the Lord said unto me, Let it suffice thee; speak no more unto me of this matter" (Deut. 3:26b).

God always hears our prayers, but He sometimes denies our requests. Moses experienced this. He prayed, "Let me go over, and see the good land that is beyond Jordan," but this request was denied. There are desires which the child of God may express in prayer and of which he need not be ashamed before God or man, which are not fulfilled.

When we read Moses' prayer, we are inclined to say that it is a good prayer. Moses lived thrice forty years to have his desire fulfilled in his life. He led the people of Israel out of Egypt, struggled through the difficulties of the desert, put up with the people's complaints and sins, and fought against the enemy. Finally Moses stood at the border of the Promised Land.

"Let me go over, and see the good land," he asked. Why shouldn't this prayer be answered positively? Many prayers of Moses had already been answered. When he prayed the waters of the Red Sea parted. When he prayed the sins of the people were forgiven. Moses was a man favored above thousands. The apostle John says: "We know that God does not hear sinners, but according to Scripture, Moses was a man who spoke with the Lord as someone speaks with a friend.

Yet his request was not granted. "Let it suffice thee; speak no more unto me of this matter," God said. The earnest desire of this great man of God was rejected. From the mountaintops he could see the waving palms of Canaan and the land flowing with milk and honey. How his heart yearned to enter! But he could not rest under the shade of the palm trees, neither could he taste anything of the fruitful land.

Moses wasn't the only one to have his request denied. Paul experienced the same thing when his prayer for the removal of the thorn in his flesh was rejected. With them there are countless other children of God who have prayed for a good cause only to have their requests denied. Indeed, there are unfulfilled prayers, prayers which have been heard, but are not granted.

Such prayers are not the same as those prayers which are sent up and the answer is a seemingly closed heaven, as was discussed in an earlier chapter. Then there was no answer and it seemed as though there was no God in heaven. Moses' prayer was clearly answered—in the negative.

One's prayer may find entrance into heaven, but his request is rejected. The one who prays notices this. He may be led to the same words spoken by God to Moses. It isn't always necessary to receive certain words from Scripture to come to the realization that a request is denied. No, the Lord also speaks in silence.

Such an experience can be as a dark cloud in the life of the child of God. Perhaps the prayer is for the healing of a child, perhaps even for the conversion of a child. It could be a prayer to have some unjust cause removed. Or it could be a prayer for peace at home or in the church. It could be for a number of things which are good in themselves.

And of course Satan is right there to use this opportunity to sow doubt. What a comfort it is for such tempted ones that even a Moses and a Paul know of unfulfilled prayers!

We can never accuse God of being unjust. Moses could not do that either, for he had made himself unworthy of having his prayer answered when he hit the rock of Meribah instead of speaking to it. Moses had given in to his sinful nature.

That is why he had nothing to say when the Lord brought back his past. He had hoped that the Lord would treat him as He did the people of Israel. When the Lord had said He would destroy His people, He was merciful and did not do so, even though they deserved to be destroyed.

Certainly God had forgiven Moses' sin. Here we see that the result of sin continues, even in the lives of God's children. It was so with David, whose sin with Bathsheba was forgiven, but the child born of sin had to die. The Lord sometimes causes the consequences of sin to remain, even though forgiveness has been granted. Thus He keeps His people humble. A bitter aftertaste is left so that the sinful past will not be forgotten. Unfulfilled prayers should shame us into silence. Let everyone consider his own Meribahs.

Is a particular sin always involved when prayers are unfulfilled? No, the Lord need not reject a prayer for a particular reason. It can happen even when there is no particular sin. But if it is not for a particular sin, then it certainly is because of *sin* that God has the right to say, "Speak no more unto me of this matter." If this doesn't bring you back to a particular "Meribah," it certainly ought to bring you back to Paradise, where *sin* began.

As we see our unworthy past we will be *kept* from rebellion and will learn to accept God's negative answers. How wonderfully this was manifested in Moses' life! We read in verse 27 that Moses climbed the mountains to see the Promised Land. He could see—but not enter. Moses did what God said. He didn't say, "Then I won't look at the land either." The Lord had said, "Let it suffice thee," and Moses said, "It suffices me." Moses ceased to speak of this matter. He climbed the mountain to see the land in the distance. Moses also received the command to charge Joshua to lead the people into the land. He would rather obey God than enter the land himself, and therefore he passed on to a successor his greatest desire.

How blessed it is to be submissive and to be united to God's will, to choose to do His will rather than to follow our own, even though it costs our dearest desire on earth! We will experience that God is sufficient for us and we will not refer to the matter again.

Our prayers may not yield the desired fruits, but they are not therefore fruitless. Unfulfilled prayers bind us to God, sometimes more than answered prayers, because those are often easily forgotten.

By unfulfilled prayers the Lord teaches His people that they must be sanctified through suffering so that they may be made to conform to the image of Christ who also has learned obedience through His suffering. Christ is the greater Moses, who not only was refused the earthly Canaan when He was cast outside the gate carrying His cross, but who was also refused the heavenly Canaan when, on the cross, He was rejected by heaven. "We bear His marks," Paul says, but Christ bore the wounds.

Not a single prayer, not even an unfulfilled prayer, sent up in sincerity, is fruitless. Often the Lord uses unfulfilled prayers. No matter how unfathomable God's ways seem, the Lord in His incomprehensible wisdom always has the eternal well-being of His Zion in mind.

This is wonderfully shown in the rejection of Moses' prayer. Shortly after this prayer Moses died and was taken up into the heavenly Canaan of eternal rest. His prayer for the earthly Canaan was rejected, but the Lord answered Moses' prayer beyond his desire and request by giving him the heavenly Canaan.

Let us for a moment imagine that Moses had received the earthly Canaan. How disappointed he would have been! For it soon became apparent that Canaan was not paradise. The complaining people underwent a change of place, but not a change of heart. They took their sin into that land. Then Moses would have had to contend with the same people and his soul would have been more grieved than when he was with them in the wilderness.

It was a heavy blow for Moses not to be allowed to enter the Promised Land. He didn't know that in this way he was spared much bitterness. God's wisdom is far greater than His child's. We may safely entrust everything to God.

Once a traveler who sat beside the coachman on a wagon grabbed the bridle when he thought that they would fall into a ravine. Instantly the coachman cruelly hit those hands. That was not kind, but if the coachman had not dealt that blow, they would have crashed into the ravine. How blessed to let go of our cause and give it into the hands of God who knows everything much better than we do.

Moses' unfulfilled prayer served to loosen his ties to the world. The Lord still does that with His people. If everything that man desires was granted, he would seek heaven on earth. But it is necessary to lose treasures here below in order to learn to lay them up on high, so that we experience more and more: "Here we have no abiding city."

If it were possible to ask Moses in heaven whether he still desired to enter the earthly Canaan, he would certainly reply, "It is sufficient; speak no more unto me of this matter." One day in these courts is better than a thousand elsewhere. How great it will be to remain there forever—forever with God—never to be without His communion. There is no greater blessing than to prepare for heaven in this life.

Unspeakably miserable are we if we know nothing of prayer—either answered or unfulfilled prayer—for that is a sign we are still going our own way. It will be terrible to fall into the hands of a God who is a stranger to us. It is far better to walk in the Lord's ways, even though that may be a deep way, than to live according to our own desires and against God's will.

There was One, greater than Moses, whose request was turned down, when as a worm He petitioned to have the cup of suffering removed from Him. When He lay wrestling He did not see the gates of Canaan but rather the gates of hell opened. In His human nature He was only a man, and what man would not beg to pass by the gates of hell? His prayer was not fulfilled. For Him it became truly: "Speak no more unto me of this matter."

12

Too Late

"And the kings of the earth and the great men, and the rich men, and the chief captains, and the mighty men, and every bondman, and every free man, hid themselves in the dens and in the rocks of the mountains; and said to the mountains and the rocks, Fall on us; and hide us from the face of him that sitteth on the throne, and from the wrath of the Lamb: For the great day of his wrath is come; and who shall be able to stand?" (Rev. 6:15-17).

These words take us to Judgment Day, that great and terrible day when the sun will be darkened and the moon become red as blood, when the stars will fall from heaven and the azure heavens will be rolled up like a scroll. Planet Earth will be moved from her place by an earthquake and there will be no safety anywhere. These are the contents of the sixth seal opened by the Lamb in Revelation. The cosmos will become chaos and a new heaven and a new earth will rise from the grave of this cursed earth. Woe to sinners who live on earth at that time and have not learned to pray. The righteous scarcely will be saved. Nevertheless, they will be surely saved and caught up into the heaven of heavens.

Let us look ahead to that time. The great Day of God's wrath has come. Christ came as a thief in the night and now the time of grace is past. Where can an unconverted sinner go now?

Sinners hide in the crevices and between the rocks, and indeed, they have fallen on their knees. Hear them pray, beg, cry, and sigh! To whom are they praying? They entreat the mountains and they implore the rocks to fall on them to crush them.

Don't they want to be saved instead of being crushed by the rocks? Yes, but that is not possible anymore. They know it too, for they say, "The great day of his wrath is come." Since they cannot stand before this wrath, they want only to be destroyed. Here the Scripture is fulfilled when it says that they will seek death but will not find it. These people cry for a death that will totally destroy them. But they cannot find such a death, because God does not undo matters and He would not be righteous if He did not punish sin.

Who are they who writhe as a worm turns itself in the dust? They are kings as well as servants, rich and poor. There is no difference between them anymore. The king lies beside the beggar and the educated beside the illiterate. In this hour they are all the same. Perhaps yesterday they despised or hated each other. Or perhaps they danced and partied together, or even sat beside each other in church. But now they all have only one prayer and that is that the mountains cover them.

Among all these desperately praying people there isn't a single one who has ever sincerely fallen down on his knees before God. There was one who would not, because he could take care of himself. Another one didn't have time; he did not control time and so time controlled him, dragging him to this terrible day. A third one had planned to change; he had had serious intentions, but they had remained intentions only. A fourth one had sought God when fear for eternity oppressed him and trouble came into his life. When the fear was gone and the trouble disappeared, he didn't pray anymore. A fifth one had often spent time in prayer, but he never admitted he was a sinner before God. His prayer had not been from the heart.

Now they all pray in dead earnest. Their prayer arises out of the depths of their hearts. It is a terrible prayer day! On their faces is written, "God is not mocked." Their prayer doesn't consist of idle words now.

How everything has changed! Maybe for twenty, forty, or even eighty years they refused to worship God. Now they crawl before dead rocks, before dead stones! Who of them would have imagined that this could happen? What a terrible plight! Now that they cannot call on the Creator anymore, they call on created matter. God had called to them in His Word: "Turn ye to me and be ye saved." But they had not done this and now they turn to the mountains for deliverance. Of course, this is foolish and they know it too. Yesterday they would have laughed if they had been told that tomorrow they would be on their knees before rocks. Man does foolish things in his despair. If only they had had more sense when help had been available!

No, the mountains cannot help them; they are only God's creation. At the most they can cover men's bodies, but not their souls. If the mountains could speak, they would say, "God is the judge who decides; you have nothing to do with us, but with God alone." Everything must obey God's command. The Creator doesn't destroy man, the crown jewel of creation, but He calls him to give an account. The Creator has a right to His creature.

This is the day of the wrath of God, and at the same time it is the day of the wrath of the Lamb. God is wrathful because of sin and the Lamb of God is wrathful because of the despising of His blood for the atonement of sin.

Who would ever think that the Lamb could be full of wrath? Isaiah says of Him that as a Lamb He was brought to the slaughter; as a defenseless, patient, long-suffering and willing Lamb. Without argument, He gave Himself to be crucified, and His mockers were allowed to do with Him what they desired. They didn't think that this Lamb could have wrath.

But now the Lamb is full of wrath. He is the same Lamb who once prayed for His enemies. The wrath of the Lamb is the counterpart of His love. Nothing is more terrible than love turned to wrath. How awful it is for those who despised His blood! "They shall look on him whom they have pierced." Then the Lamb will say, "Slay them before my feet, those who would not have me as their king." We cannot say death is death, because it will be an eternal death. The ones who pray to the mountains know this, for they desire the temporal death of the mountains in order to escape eternal death. They themselves say that this is the wrath of the Lamb. They wouldn't have known this if the Lamb had not been preached to them. They knew a time when the grace of Christ was offered to them. They heard the voice of Jesus when He cried, "Whosoever cometh unto me I will in no wise cast out." Their sin and Christ's grace was pointed out to them. They knew that there was a mediator to save sinners, but they would not come to Him.

Some of these people never engaged in secret prayer. They did not need God and Christ and worship. The world was much more attractive to them than the church. They even thought they were honest when they said, "If you have no desire for those things, it is only hypocrisy to go to church, and at least I'm not a hypocrite."

Others had an easy religion. They thought they had no need for a close relationship with the Lord, because after all, Jesus died for sinners. They never bothered to find out how a sinner becomes united to Christ. Their religion was merely outward.

And then there were those who took religion very seriously. They were not offended when eternal damnation was preached. They were even fervent in telling others about the coming judgment. But with all their zealousness they never wept a tear for the sins they committed against God. Their religion too, was merely outward.

Do you belong to one of these classes of people? Will you one day cry out in vain when the day of grace is ended? If you lead a prayerless life it is hard to realize that one day you will seek death and will not find it. You will turn to prayer then, but your prayers will be to the mountains. If you don't now become concerned with the question, "Who shall stand before His wrath?" you will become concerned when it is too late.

We will all meet the Lamb of God in one way or another. Either we are covered with the blood of the Lamb now or we will meet with the wrath of the Lamb later. Why, then, don't you bow down before God now? It is foolish to continue as if there is no God in heaven and no eternity that awaits us. "The fool," says Scripture, "says in his heart that there is no God." There is no more foolish person than one who doesn't pray.

"But," says someone, "you cannot pray unless it is given from above." True, but how do you know that? Do you know that by experience? Or, have you heard others say it? And when you cannot pray, how does that affect you? Has that brought you to say along with the disciples: "Lord, teach me to pray"? If you are not troubled by your inability to pray, you, too, are foolish.

Think about the privileges you have. Perhaps you have been brought up with the doctrines of God's Word since you were a child. Maybe you have a praying father or mother. Maybe you also have had prayer for material things answered. And yet with all this are you still a stranger to God and therefore lost?

Do not have harsh thoughts of God. The Lord did not bestow all these privileges on you to condemn you; He has no pleasure in your condemnation. He bestowed all these blessings on you that you might come to Him and find salvation in His Son.

While He proffers peace and pardon
Let us hear His voice today,
Lest, if we our hearts should harden,
We should perish in the way.

Those who have communion with God in secret will not be put to shame in the day of days. The Lord knows those who are His, even though they may feel they are not known by Him. The mark by which they are known is prayer.

There are many different kinds of prayer.

Secret prayer may be just a sighing after God. Often this sighing is not associated with words, a form, time, or place. True prayer is not bound to outward forms; what matters is the heart.

Persevering prayer occurs when the sinner experiences the darkness of a closed heaven, and yet would rather perish than let go of God.

Humble prayer is when a person bows so deeply before God that he recognizes only two possibilities: death or grace. Here a sinner truly recognizes his sinfulness.

Bold prayer goes with humility because boldness is found in Christ and not in the one who prays. Only the humble have this boldness.

True prayer is worked by the Spirit of prayer. He inclines the heart to conform to the will of God and He helps the weaknesses of those who pray with wordless groanings so that they receive only what is good for them.

Pleading prayer is exercised when one who knows he has no rights has a pleading ground outside of himself, which is the name of the Redeemer and Savior, Jesus Christ.

Fervent prayer is prayer that acknowledges God for all His goodness and especially for the gift—Christ—in whom all temporal and spiritual benefits are found.

Unfulfilled prayer often teaches more than answered prayer because God uses it to draw the sinner to Himself so that blessings are given above and beyond the expectation of prayer.

No one will be saved because of any worthiness in prayer itself. Christians are no better than those who will cry to the mountains and the rocks. People will not be saved because they began with God, but as a result of His electing love. Therefore prayer cannot give any merit before God. Those who pray will certainly arrive at their desired haven because salvation is God's own work. He will bring people—from the greatest to the smallest—to Himself.

Only one kind of prayer will continue into eternity. That is the prayer of adoration of the Triune God—God the Father, the source of prayer; God the Son, the ground of prayer; and God the Spirit, the effectual power of prayer.